purplēdeneye

Also by Michael H. Kew

Crossings (2012)
Rainbownesia (2019)
Nectars of Sky (2020)

purplēdeneye

Michael H. Kew

Spruce Coast Press

Spruce Coast Press
Curry County, Oregon

michaelkew.com
@michael.kew

U.S. Library of Congress Cataloging-in-Publication Data
Identifiers: LCCN 2020923530 | ISBN 9780997508567 (pbk.)
Author, American–21st century | Poetry, Dreams, Nature, Consciousness, Metaphysics
LOC record available at http://lccn.loc.gov/2020923530

Designed by Sarah M. Reed
Front cover & frontispiece by Spencer Reynolds 2020
Pink Moon over Mount Emily image by the author April 2020
Milky Way from Vulcan Lake by David Lovell July 2020
Author portrait by Glencora Powers March 2020
Back cover NEOWISE comet from Stump Prairie by David Lovell July 2020

Manufactured in the United States of America
First Edition

Inside the dream, button sleep around your body like a glove.
Free now of space and time. Free to dissolve in the streaming summer....
Sleep is an under-ocean dipped into each night.
At morning, awake dripping, gasping, eyes stinging....
In the womb we are blind cave fish.

—Jim Morrison, *The Lords*

CONTENTS

LEXICS

Abecedarian An alphabetical acrostic in which each line or stanza begins with a successive letter of the alphabet. (Edward Hirsch, *A Poet's Glossary*)

Acronymic Verse in which the letters of a given word furnish the initials of the words used in each line. (Harry Mathews, *Oulipo Compendium*)

Acrostic A vertical succession of letters that, in a series of lines or verses, forms a word, name, or phrase. (Mathews)

Addition A text is altered through several iterations by adding letters, spaces, and punctuation. (William Gillespie, *Table of Forms*)

Ae freislighe (Literally "lying down poetry") is one of the most common forms of Irish verse. Four lines to each stanza, with seven syllables in each line. Lines 1 and 3 employ a three syllable end-rhyme, while lines 2 and 4 use a two syllable end-rhyme. The final syllable of the poem should be the same as the first syllable. (Connor Sansby, Thanet Writers)

Alphabet Different ways to write an alphabet poem: the first letter of each word is a different letter of the alphabet; consecutively through the alphabet; through the alphabet using the first letter of the first word for each line; flip the alphabet—instead of A to Z, from Z to A. (Robert Lee Brewer, Writer's Digest)

Anagram Greek: "transposition of letters." A word or phrase rearranged to form another word or phrase. (Hirsch)

Anterhyme Lines of a poem where the rhyme falls on their first syllables rather than their last. (Mathews)

Ballad The traditional British ballad is a narrative song, a poem that tells a story, preserved and transmitted orally. It unfolds in four-line stanzas and customarily alternates four- and three-stress lines. The second and fourth lines rhyme. (Hirsch)

Boolean *[As in George Boole, 19th-century English mathematician who first defined an algebraic system of logic.]* Boolean Logic is a form of algebra which is centered around three simple words known as Boolean Operators: "Or," "And," and "Not". At the heart of Boolean Logic is the idea that all values are either true or false. (Lotame Solutions)

Chronogram Exploits the double significance of those letters that are also Roman numerals: *i, v, x, l, c, d*, and *m*. When such letters are identified in a chronogram and added up according to their numerical value, their sum will correspond to a given year of the Christian era. (Mathews)

Clerihew Comic poetry...consists of a skewed quatrain—two rhyming couplets (*aabb*) of unequal length that whimsically encapsulate a person's biography. The form spoofs metrical smoothness. There is usually something ludicrous in the deadpan send-up of a famous person whose name appears as one of the rhymed words in the first couplet. (Hirsch)

Conovowel Alternates vowels and consonants. (Gillespie)

Cywydd llosgyrnog (Emerging in the 14th century) the Cywydd is perhaps the most important of (Welsh) forms. It was highly favored by the Poets of the Nobility (Cywyddwyr) and often used to praise the land-owning patrons. Unlike many forms of cywydd, there is a fixed length to a cywydd llosgyrnog. They are strictly sestets (six lined poems) and feature a complex, interlocking rhyme scheme. The first couplet has eight syllables. This is followed by a seven-syllable line, featuring a cross-rhyme with the first couplet on either the third or fourth syllable. Another couplet follows with eight syllables and a new rhyme, followed by a final line of seven syllables with a cross-rhyme again on the third or fourth syllable and a final rhyme coupled with the previous cross-rhyming line. (Sansby)

Diamond A combined snowball and melting snowball, a poem with a regular increase in the number of letters per line followed by a corresponding decrease...known as a diamond poem because of the shape it makes when centered on the page. (Gillespie)

Epigram From the Greek *epigramma*, "to write upon"...a short, witty poem or pointed saying. It has no particular form, though it often employs a rhymed couplet or quatrain. (Hirsch)

Epitaph Greek: "on a tomb"...can be either a commemorative short poem inscribed on a gravestone or a poem that imitates one. The imitative type creates the fiction of a memorial site. (Hirsch)

Etheree (double reverse) Ten lines of unmetered and unrhymed verse, the first line having one syllable and each succeeding line adding a syllable...the total syllable count being 55. It goes in chronological order on the lines corresponding to the amount of syllables on it. It is a successive one-to-one system...can also go in reverse. A double etheree is a 20-line poem. (Poetry Soup)

Fib The number of syllables in each line equals the total number of syllables in the preceding two lines. The Fibonacci sequence begins with either zero or one, followed by one, and proceeds based on the rule that each number—called a Fibonacci number—is equal to the sum of the preceding two numbers. (Poetry Society of Indiana)

Ghazal Originally an Arabic verse form dealing with loss and romantic love, medieval

Persian poets embraced the ghazal, eventually making it their own. Consisting of syntactically and grammatically complete couplets, the form also has an intricate rhyme scheme. Each couplet ends on the same word or phrase (the *radif*), and is preceded by the couplet's rhyming word (the *qafia*, which appears twice in the first couplet). The last couplet includes a proper name, often of the poet's. In the Persian tradition, each couplet was of the same meter and length, and the subject matter included both erotic longing and religious belief or mysticism. (Poetry Foundation)

Ginsist [See explanation on poem page.]

Haibun Connects individual haiku with a surrounding prose narrative. (Hirsch)

Haikuisation The haiku is a Japanese poetic form whose most obvious feature is the division of its 17 syllables into lines of 5, 7, and 5 syllables. Haikuisation has sometimes been used by Oulipians to indicate the reduction of verses of normal length to lines of haiku-like brevity. (Mathews)

Irrational sonnet A 14-line sonnet divided according to the first five digits of the irrational number π (pi); that is, into stanzas of 3, 1, 4, 1, and 5 lines. The two one-line stanzas are best treated as refrains, having their rhyme-word and other words in common. There are four rhymes, distributed thus: *aab c baab c cdccd*. (Mathews)

Isonym A text that does not repeat a word. (Gillespie)

Jeremiad A lamentation, a doleful complaint, a sustained invective. The jeremiad, named after the prophet Jeremiah, is a long literary work, usually in prose, sometimes in poetry. (Hirsch)

Khamriyyat Medieval Arabic poets had a lively genre of wine poetry...derived from the social institution of wine parties...numerous thematic possibilities. (Hirsch)

Kyrielle A French form of rhyming poetry written in quatrains (a stanza consisting of 4 lines), and each quatrain contains a repeating line or phrase as a refrain (usually appearing as the last line of each stanza). Each line within the poem consists of only eight syllables. (Shadow Poetry)

Limerick A fixed light-verse form of five generally anapestic lines rhyming *aabba*. Edward Lear, who popularized the form, fused the third and fourth lines into a single line with internal rhyme. Limericks are traditionally bawdy or just irreverent. (Poetry Foundation)

Lipogram A text that excludes one or more letters of the alphabet. The ingenuity demanded by the restriction clearly varies in proportion to the frequency of the letter or letters excluded. (Mathews)

Luc-bat Vietnamese: "six-eight"...alternates lines of six and eight syllables in tightly rhymed couplets....Each rhyme recurs three times: at the end of the first eight-syllable line, at the end of the next six-syllable line, and as the sixth syllable of the next eight-syllable line. (Hirsch)

Melting snowball A text in which each word has one letter less than the preceding one, and the last word only one letter. (Mathews)

Mesostic A poem or other typographical arrangement in which a vertical word or phrase intersects lines of horizontal texts. (Hirsch)

N+7 A method invented by Jean Lescure that "consists" (in [Raymond] Queneau's terse definition) "in replacing each noun (N) with the seventh following it in a dictionary".... The texts treated can be original or not, distinguished or undistinguished, prose or verse. (Mathews)

Nocturne A night scene....In early church writings, the French term nocturnes refers to "night prayer" or night vigil...associating night with spiritual contemplation...one could make a good international anthology of the modern poetic nocturne, which is frequently a threshold poem that puts us in the presence of nothingness or God – it returns us to origins – and stirs poets toward song. (Hirsch)

Nonet A nine-line poem that has nine syllables in the first line, eight syllables in the second line, seven syllables in the third line, and continues to count down to one syllable in the final line. (Brewer)

Oligogrammatic Only the letters of (a common) phrase can be used. The phrase itself invariably constitutes the first line of the poem, which thus becomes a commentary on it. Most of the phrases chosen...are highly idiomatic and resist succinct translation. (Mathews)

Ottava rima Originally an Italian stanza of eight 11-syllable lines with a rhyme scheme of abababcc. Lord Byron adapted it to a 10-syllable line. (Poetry Foundation)

Palindrome A text of indeterminate length whose letters can be read both forwards and backwards. (Mathews)

Pangram A sentence that uses all the letters of the alphabet. (Hirsch)

Pantoum A Malaysian verse form adapted by French poets and occasionally imitated in English. It comprises a series of quatrains, with the second and fourth lines of each quatrain repeated as the first and third lines of the next. The second and fourth lines of the final stanza repeat the first and third lines of the first stanza. (Poetry Foundation)

Quatorzain From the French *quatorze*, "fourteen"...an anamorphic or abortive poem or sonnet. It consists of 14 lines and is, like a sonnet, divided into two tercets and two quatrains. (Language is a Virus)

Quenina Sestina-like poems with stanzas of different lengths. No end-words occupy the same position twice...(only) with a select group of numbers, the first few being: 1, 2, 3, 5, 6, 9, 11, 14, and 18. (Philip Terry, *The Penguin Book of Oulipo*) [My quenina herein is a five-stanza, five-line quintina.]

Rann Four-line stanza in Irish verse. The early Irish poets had rigorous rules for creating stanzas. One primary type divided the quatrain into two parts. The initial couplet was called the *Seoladh*, or the leading couplet, the second the *Comhad*, or the closing couplet. Each rann was a self-contained unit. (Hirsch)

Rhopalic Also known as a wedge verse or (syllabic snowball) verse. The word *rhopalic* comes from the Greek rhopalos, meaning "clublike" or "cudgel," something that expands or thickens toward the end. Each word or group of words is one syllable longer than the one that precedes it. (Hirsch)

Sestanagramina Version of sestina wherein every word is an anagram from the poem's title. (Oulipo)

Tanka One of the oldest Japanese forms...a 31-syllable poem traditionally written in a single unbroken line. A form of *waka*, Japanese song or verse, *tanka* translates as "short song" and is better known in its five-line, 5/7/5/7/7 syllable count form. Like the sonnet, the tanka employs a turn, known as a pivotal image, which marks the transition from the examination of an image to the examination of the personal response. This turn is located within the third line, connecting the *kami-no-ku*, or upper poem, with the *shimo-no-ku*, or lower poem. (Academy of American Poets)

Tautogram A text whose words, or at least the principal ones, all begin with the same letter. (Mathews)

Tetractys "Euclid, the (Greek) mathematician of classical times, considered the number series *1, 2, 3, 4* to have mystical significance because its sum is 10, so he dignified it with a name of its own: tetractys. The tetractys could be Britain's answer to the haiku. Its challenge is to express a complete thought, profound or comic, witty or wise, within the narrow compass of 20 syllables." —Ray Stebbing (tetractys inventor)

Univocalic A text written with a single vowel; it is consequently a lipogram in all the other vowels. (Mathews)

Villanelle A French form codified in the 16th century....19 lines divided into six stanzas—five tercets and one quatrain. The first and third lines become the refrain lines of alternate stanzas and the final two lines of the poem. They rhyme throughout, as do the middle lines of each stanza. The entire poem then builds around two repeated lines and turns on two rhymes. (Hirsch)

Wasf Literary term meaning "description;" but it can carry several other connotations, including "quality," "attribute," "characterization," "distinguishing mark," and "adjective," which are also relevant to the analysis of descriptive poetry in Persian.... in a specific context, the poet or the critic using the term may have one or all of these meanings and connotations in mind. Waṣf passages serve different purposes in different genres and poetic forms. (*Encyclopædia Iranica*)

X mistakes Y for Z The relation *x mistakes y for z* was conceived by [Oulipian] Raymond Queneau as a way of representing the way that several characters perceive each other (and themselves) in a given situation. The relationship *x* mistakes *y* for *z* can be extended to attitudes, sentiments, or actions other than a knowledge of identity. (Mathews)

Yuugen A multivalent and influential medieval aesthetic ideal expressing darkness, depth, mystery, transience, ambiguity, calm, sadness, and elegance. The term originated in China as *youxuan* and meant Daoist or Buddhist truth beyond intellectual comprehension. (*Dictionary of Japanese Architectural and Art Historical Terminology*)

Zéjel A Spanish poetic form...begins with an introductory stanza, a brief initial *estribillo* (refrain) that presents the theme of the poem. This is followed by a tercet, which is called a *mudanza* (changing verse) with a single rhyme (*monorrimo*). The mudanza, which at times also had internal rhymes, is followed by the repetition of one or more lines, a *vuelta*—"turn" or "return"—rhyming with the initial stanza. Typically written in eight-syllable lines. (Hirsch)

PROLEGOMENON

Twenty-twenty was to be my fat fertile year pimping *Rainbownesia* and *Nectars of Sky*. Myriad sales, signings, readings, slams, fests—months of general gaiety and hobnob abundance spanning the U.S. West Coast, British Columbia, Hawai'i, points Atlantic, aims of Europe and the Trans-Tasman. For me, an ambivert weaving a pseudomonastic life in the coastal mountains of southern Oregon, the books promised a depth of opportunity, a rejuvenating social manifest. Four author appearances occurred in late winter. Then the world shut down.

By April I'd begun chronicling fragments of my increasingly vivid dream journeys, not deliberately to craft new works but to interpret per curiosity as most were quite lively and communal—a sharp contrast to the wacky anthroreality unfolding. Subconsciously I was living vigorously. There were no lockdowns, no hint of face masks nor hand sanitizing-six feeting-societal suffocating-quagmired quarantining. Rather: smiles, laughter, wild parties, music concerts, beach gatherings, pubbing, womening, world traveling, odd yet delightful scenarios—my nocturnality depicted merry normality while 2020 burst into a wide dinurnal stink of nightmare.

One rainy May dusk with a glass of Humboldt petite sirah, I browsed my new copy of *The Penguin Book of Oulipo*, a lush 400-page anthology of exotic poetic structures and techniques exemplifying the Oulipo, or *Ouvroir de Littér hature Potentielle* (Workshop of Potential Literature), founded in 1960 by writer Raymond Queneau and mathematician François Le Lionnais, two brilliant Frenchmen who elected unique individuals into what became a small eccentric core of giant minds. One, Jacques Roubaud, summarized Oulipo thus: "The aim is to invent (or reinvent) constraints of a formal nature and propose them to enthusiasts interested in composing literature." New York-based Academy of American Poets boiled Oulipo doctrine down to "the profound potential of a poem produced within a framework or formula and that, if done in a playful posture, the outcomes could be endless."

To that end(less?), equipped also with cherished copies of Harry Mathews's *Oulipo Compendium* (an Oulipo dictionary), William Gillespie's weirdo Oulipoish *Table of Forms*, and Edward Hirsch's iconic *A Poet's Glossary*, spontaneously I resolved to distill my waxing collection of dream notes, eventually whittling 55 of them into 55 poems per 55 structures, 55 a Fibonacci number (indeed the works in *Nectars of Sky* totaled 89, successive in that sacred sequence).

Whereas—

Sequentially, dreams sing sweetly for but a few years inside of us. Recollected or not, in the average human lifespan we drift through enigmas several times nightly (or daily, depending), most individual dreams lasting from five to 20 minutes and never in exclusive grayscale as once believed.

Hence—

Eternal queri: why do we dream? what are dreams? why do we dream what we dream? why do we dream what we dream when we dream? what do dreams mean, if anything? does it matter? do we care? should we care? are they antiphonic duels—or harmonies—'twixt consciousnesses? psycho-anaphora? quasi-psychedelia? hallucination? prophetic déjà vu? (like many of mine.)

Here in the West, British neurowhiz Oliver Sacks failed to divine these mysteries. He and others published serious tomes, studies, essays, pontifications, analyses. And to what end? Austria's Freud proffered meat with his holy trinity (id, ego, superego) as personal wish-fulfillment, dreams our "royal road to the unconscious." Per individuation, Freud pupil Jung the Swiss implied dreams were missives from the inner (unconscious) to the outer (conscious) worlds however they corresponded with each other.

Both men fleshed a mind-scale of four tiers:

conscious fueled by ego

preconscious data at the ego's disposal

personal unconscious instinct; Freud's id

collective unconscious Jung's "vast historical storehouse of the human race"

Via the latter and quite similarly, German psychiatrist/psychotherapist Fritz Perls employed his own gestalt ("form" or "pattern") theory, i.e. the whole of anything is greater than its parts, e.g. dreams are neglected cogs of

17

our psyche and issues repressed by awake time. Whiffs of rhythmic logic and reality could be glued to recurring topics and scenarios based on conscious emotions and occurrences when our thought channels are laid bare, our brains unleashed from external influence—multivalent motifs pursuing cross-psychic dimensions.

Modernly, American psychiatrist-psychoanalyst J. Allan Hobson and British neuroscientist Karl Friston hatched a plausible fact-heavy hypothesis: based on your dreambrain activity during REM (rapid eye movement) cycles, overall it is a simulation device crafting a virtual reality of your waked environs. And so, through the hole of my REM iris churned unforeseen holographic visions/truisms, often forgotten upon or shortly after I woke, the breathlessly bizarre, the serene, even the disturbing ephemera that I sought to record and decipher for their amaranthine omens. Or provenance. Or zaniness. Or, more empiric, for their 20/20 nowsights.

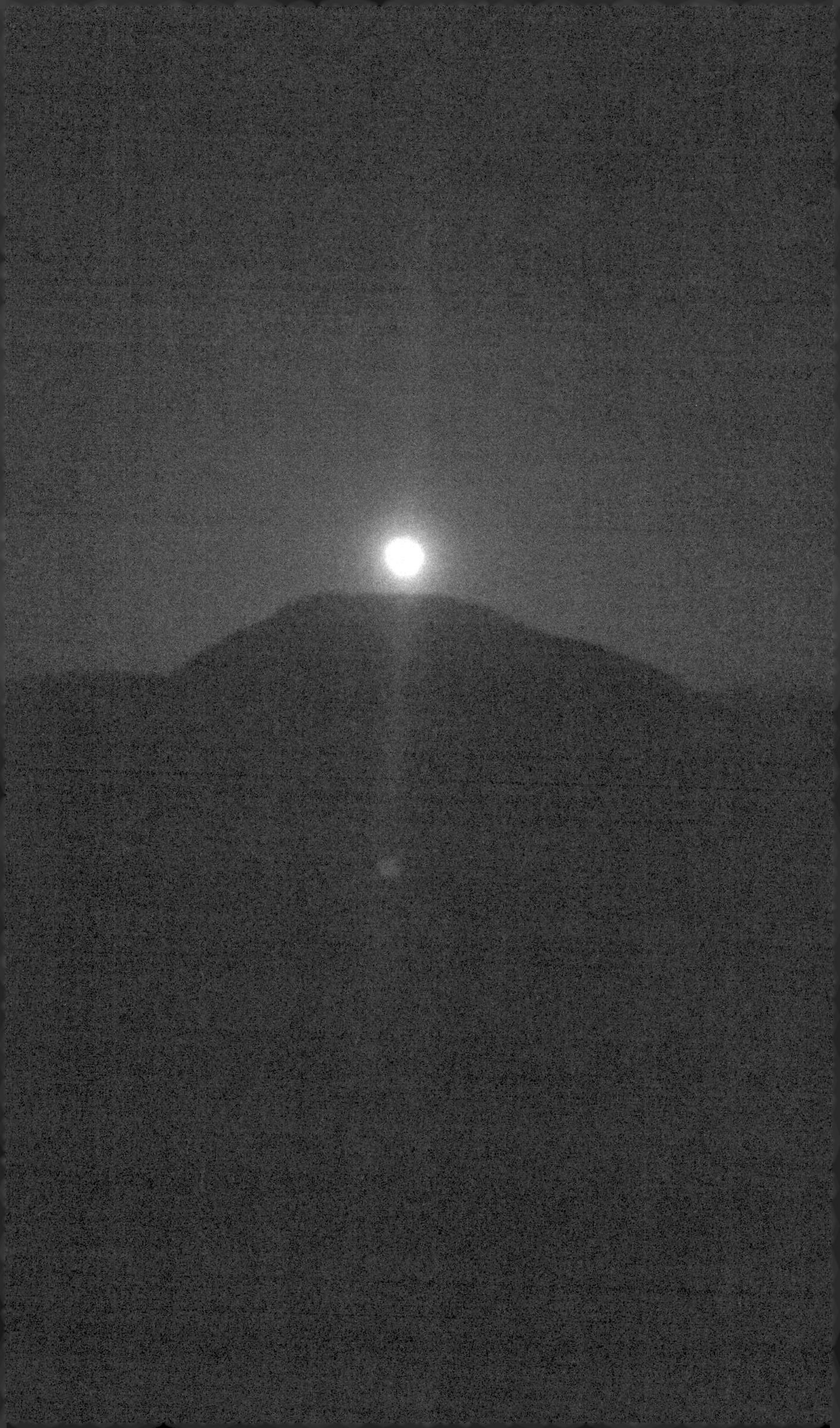

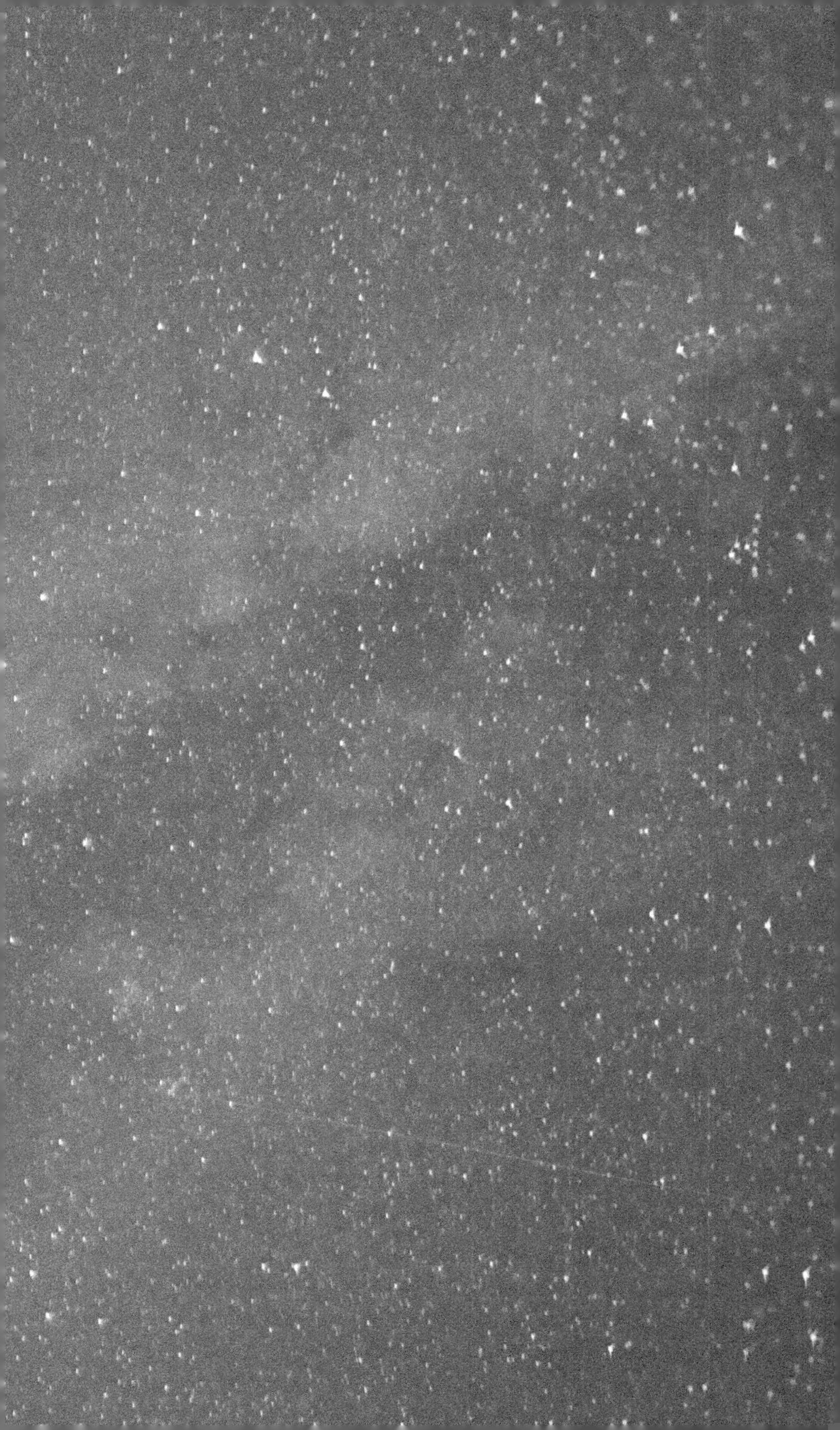

Mandala Tears

abecedarian

Am pulled over

By an old yellow rusted Volkswagen Rabbit

Car/pickup with rooftop sirens that

Deceivingly look like wood pallets—

Excited when out—zop!—steps a voluptuous

Fashionable young blonde in tight very short white

Gown or dress and wearing silver watch on

Her wrist above

Impressible soft hand of slender fingers holding some sort of clear plastic

Jigger and she

Kindly suggests I use it to test my prostate—I do not know where it is

Located nor why and I tell her it is always

Magnificence to be

Noticed by a beautiful woman—she swirls 'round and

Orbits back to plant a wet kiss on my dry dry lips in the wind—

Previously I am exiting a college building and I hold the door open for a

Quizzical girl who I

Recognize from a class I did not attend—a pretty boho chic turquoise jewelled

Surfer, very tender, and she too kisses me—

Timidly I open my eyes and she is a he—

Undulating emotions for these desirous

Vixens, passions I no feel for longtime lust as I lay

Warmly listening to soft rustlings of rainings seeping into my

Xeriscape of parched heart aside dreaming felines on purple sheetings in

dark bedroom—

Zealous mandala tears 'twixt blackout curtains—edging the cloudbleeds

of bluefuzz bliss

Hermit

acronymic

Hoedown eastward Rincon; musician is twanging
Hidden embers rekindle magical inner tingles
Halycon eons rewound; missus' idyllic thoughts
Harsh existential reality—McCann is transposed
His exiting Rincon momentarily invites transition
Heated early rainfree May, iridescent time
Hollow eaves remain molded in tune
Heartfelt excursions resonate mostly internally, tragically
Heavy emotional residue marks important turnaround
Humid endings ready; Mobile is touching
Hauling enthusiastic Ronin miles, interstate tenderness
Hidden easygoing roots—mandatory, it teaches

Homing eagerness revealed Mercy's implied thirst
Her energy represented myriad improvisational talents
Heartbroken—erotic reruns, my intense theatre
Headstrong eagerness railroaded my impetuous tenacity
Humorless ending reopened midnight's icy trauma
Holy evenings rendered moving inspirational tendency
Highway eyes, rural Massachusetts intact, 2 a.m.

Hilarious enduring relief, mate's intelligent toasts
His elevated realism multiplied innocent trust
Heavenly epiphanic rapturous meditation isn't taradiddle
Healthy everything, rug muggy, insignificant township
Hard elixirs reduce mindful intuition tradition
Hangovers excruciatingly rawboned, mindless ingested toxin
Haunted elementary rituals manifests immature termination
Honey earth reappears moonlit, introducing tranquility
Happy eternal remembrances—mellifluous infinite truths

Barbed Heart

acrostic

Mentally masturbating and blinking in dens of dread
Exacerbating midlife crises via pandemic hysteric
Lack of work or want or will as wee-hour rains wane
Air is again silent and irradiated by cosmochemists
Nettling tinnitus ensnares my wandering skull
Cats purr and knead beneath celestial salvation
Heart beats in my belly as I rise to plead with Pink Moon
Outside my window, white-crowned sparrow sings
Lovebird in madrone or fir or tanoak
Isolatingly aching in early waking and thinking
About people who are surely not thinking about you

Mind Meadows

addition

gently licking moonshine from a splintery stick.

gin-telling my lucky groom bride to curl from ass-splendid terry stick.

a stiff cuppa gin for William Tell(ing), gently wedded in gloomy groom pride to
my bride with the apple curls licking lucky moonshine from her arrowglass ass,
terroir for a splendid splintery stick.

Weeneolith

ae freislighe

Sun-greased midday Kettletoft
I'm walking a bike uphill
Been sweating nuts eversoft
Aside peat bay of windchill

Atop curls of cleanliness
Drop down wave face, shore rocky
Thin white streak towards Tankerness
Small remote-controlled surfer—stocky

Lilliputian Nazaré
White streak really is fishing—
Line, it drags, not surfari
Pole gripped by stout man wishing

He is Robert Trujillo
Mex Metallica bassist
With iPhone-sized burrito
Blefuscudian playlist

He pushes *Play* suddenly
Lifts a sword, sharp and shiny
Becomes black fish, luckily
As my skin becomes slimy

Now Robert be vomiting—
Burrito of fish rancid
Surf starts to look promising
Over Orkney reef slanted

Puke pile pic for Instagram
Sun Ra toots from Rob's speaker—
As 'likes' flow from Pakistan
Phone falls as he grows weaker

I wonder 'bout Eynhallow
The wind is shifting southeast
Rob asks for a wheelbarrow
Before he is soon deceased

Vernal Humm

alphabet

zooming young xantus' wings vibrate under tiny schoolkids
reluctantly quarantined,
playtime obstructed, neighborly mandated lockdowns, kisses jeopardized,
independence halted, general freedoms enjoined despite cute birds airborne

Silhouette

anagram

The lotus oil tousles from his lithe holiest toe slits,
It shines to these hottest hotlist hues—
Oh, hi, sole lust!
Oh—soul?
This lets ethos lose to its steel silt toilets
Oi!
Let us shout lost shots to shut the hostile hostel holes
Thou lush tush to shit out eel isles
Hoist teal hose south to heels to stout thistle house
Lo!
He settles—uh—shuttles loutish sleuths to use tile teeth to see lie suites
Tie his shoes to use those elite sleet hosts, eh?
Thus, it is shit oil

Root Rot

anterhyme

Ski suits are worn by Nick and Ross – illogical on this tropical isle –
Passionfruit drips from Nick's yellow walrus mustache of bleached sail horizons
– En route to the hills, we stop the car at an apartment on a night college-
town street – Absolute confusion after we enter and two boys ask: *What the
fuck you looking at?* – Prostitutes flee the red-lighted room – all but one,
a brunette – Birthday suit is admired as her plan to go diving (not skiing) is
devised – Swimsuits are donned and we end up at a big party of underground
community – Irresolute and shy, I see a blonde I had just matched with on
Bumble – Disrepute with such apps manifests in the revealing of her fleshly
uncomeliness – Attributed to ancient imagery added aka false advertising
Substituted this interaction with a raucous gathering 'round a table of Vegas
lobsters – Hirsute mood strikes and I start to crack jokes and many revelers shift
forward and back – Recruits all to view a big long map of Pacific islands unfurled
on the sticky floor – Grapefruit juice is what Ross has mixed with his jug of
vodka that he pushes at me – Resolute, I refuse and insist I am not always sober
– Uprooted is my inclusion beneath the bright sweaty lights above a comfortable
couch – Disputed are odds of actually going diving or even snorkeling with
prostitutes – Electrocuted becomes the rowdy scene as sad lonely Maylight bleeds

Didgeridoo Lung

ballad

Hiking with two or three surfers
I don't know who
In a rawdust spring desert
Middle Baja, perhaps, or Gnaraloo

Maybe bright sandswept Jalama
Its hot squeak sands of cowpoke ranch
We are inside a pebbly black drainpipe
Where I fear a shale avalanche

We tear the pipe's top wide open
And rush down this ocean cliff
Suddenly we're agape over hellish reefs
All made of smoking spliffs

"Fire!" someone yells to the glare
While in the tube, somebody stalls
While somebody is ecstatic to the brown sky
Ninety inches of snow shall fall

Withershins Kalifornia

Boolean

If I'm to paddle a surfboard from Frisco to Crescent City
With no wetsuit nor food nor water
Will I be greeted by a Point Arena shark subcommittee?
Will King Newsom surveil my slaughter?

"Maybe I can stroke north wearing just blue latex gloves,"
I say to Miki Dora as we feed some doves
On guano-caked rocks just past the Golden Gate
I ask if he'd like to help me search for lost pieces-of-eight

He says no 'cept suddenly we're beached, arid and hot
Watching 18 surfers hound small green left-handers
Must be where they grow pounds of legal pot
'cept to naked tweakers licking orange salamanders

Miki vanishes, or maybe he gets smoked
Stuffed into huge rolling papers not soaked
Now the surfers are all fishing for sharks
I tell them about my life in Shelter Cove, mowing parks

But four of them do not want to hear my old rusty tale
And then I'm in some townhouse, greeted by two beautiful women
One is joking with me and she has a nice ass, plump and pale
She wears white spandex shorts and offers me gin with lemon

I assume she is Miki's girlfriend, except Miki is now Ryan Burch
She is drunk and tells me she never drinks, instead preferring church
She pukes into Ryan's hair while he plays video games on the curb
But he's now Jessie from the Cove, surfarmer of sweet herb

Then I'm with family in San Diego in my grandmother's holy kitchen
Someone yells "Merry Christmas!" and "Would you like to pitch in?"
Church bells gong and Jessie leaps away, screaming "Yum blanc!"
Grandma wipes her Rudolph sweater as an elk horn now honks

I quiver with anxiety and my gut balloons with dread
I hear her unique voice crisply, except she is dead
She piles homecooked food 12 inches high on my plate
But look!–
Indeed I've paddled to the wrong side of the state

Lost Quaffed Peat

chronogram

— gazing at goats in an Ethiopian zoo
— a rusty phone rings
— Alex DR waxes from Houston but he's fibbing
— he's on Tortola, where he luxuriates
— says he's boxing in prison
— strange to hear his British after 20 years of not
— he in Cornwall, I in Garberville, grieving = 2020

Metal Rhathymia

clerihew

James Hetfield's flaxen 'stache
Spit-soaked in '80s "Whiplash"
Says he'll buy my guitar-shaped surfboard
If I'll jig-dance naked to "Phantom Lord"

Fever Dreams

conovowel

he was an imaginative academic
an aged aloha man of america line
he arose on monotone sun time
developed, waxed, waned
deliberately wizened in vocabulary validity
dedicated to get recovery of humanity
a rare isolated ego
to everybody a paradoxical pet animal
an elite ace to operate a marine life
made busy to simulate civility on every face
cute women examined and adored his sex ceremony
timely lure of delicate monogamy
fake ability to cogitate and generalize
to maximize his pirate image
a mix of repose, music, power
power to make love a literature
a page to poke, to rebuke, to eliminate
to mimic and deify and date hot females
a base-level of unlimited love
a dire mix of separate motives to modulate hate
but a diminutive devil virus rode his nose
now aloha man is remote
an alohaloser
a zany baby
a raw nobody
an american love kamikaze

Limn the Love

cywydd llosgyrnog

cyan surfglow Caribbean
wet-bar duskvibe Creoles creepin'
your Czech nectarean friend
she's smothered by drug dealer's fart
he's four-capped through aortic chart
handgunned heart like John Lennon's

Dora Lives

diamond

sun
blithe, chirpy
throttling, flushing, smiling
life, euphoria, death, melancholia
aging, killing, vanishing
panicky, sickly
moon

Panic Porn

epigram

Near-distance instant authoritarianism
Fearmongering—mental mass terrorism
Civil liberties—sudden outlaws
Uncle Sam—redfat as Santa Claus

Beaver Bones

epitaph

Drought for months, winter a hoax
Guzzling beer, I'm admiring folks
Sky summery, a day for meadow
Chetco lowflowing tragic woeful
By nightfall I lay aside old woodshed
Battling riverbitches who wish me dead

After Emerald

etheree

At a corner stop where there is a creek
or river rushing past and people
are milling about and I walk
into a building that looks
of log and I learn we
shall float downriver
with these girls I
am texting—
dating
apps—
the
river
beautiful
dark jade flying
softly like butter
through shin-split riffle in
the shade of tanoaks and I
consider my kayak and we
long laze afloat in euphoria—
pluck aquatic 'shrooms for Victoria

Rainbow Garden

fib

ø
a
small
airport
on Kauai—
I squat on the mud
at the arrivals area
to collect someone amid extremely heavy rain
at night / I see Jenny, a lush Seattle brunette featured in my previous dream—
a tryst to unwrap in San Diego where she'd retrieved me from its airport and
wheeled my soggy hangover straight to the old Waterfront

where we beersauced and greased our lust faces with hamburgers and she
drunkdrove us to her house early-morning / later that day and for the next
three my parents and I further feasted at Marie Callender's in Olivenhain.

my younger sister Kirstie was there too debating either racism or sexism
and I overheard from a television: "oh, that's not true, and these gyms are
everywhere!" : and began wonder if in fact I had been with Jenny whose hair
was so brown it was almost black and in fact that was the last time I would see
her—but—wasn't she named Zemina? so long ago.

into my goopy potato brainfog my flaccid spinal cord surged with electric
excrement and intrigue and desire and comfort with a morsel of challenge
/ high at a brewpub with someone unknown I slouched at the bar's corner
overlooking a bunch of people and I felt embarrassed to be there because one
of the staff plus the girl I saw in the Kauai airport (she was never seen again)
had watched me piss so much piss it was a cornucopian yellow monsoon pissfall
from airport gutters where it was actually sunny and I've yet to visit the isle.

0, 1, 1, 2, 3, 5, 8, 13, 21, 34, 55, 89, 144

Somewhat, Epizeuxis

ghazal

Some sort of juicy desperation—moons bursting with dark serenity,
Buttered black dwarf in my skull smelling pearls of heated serenity.

Crowded movie theater where people run sideways to sun destinies,
Plates of cold Chinese food at every seat; I sit in depleted serenity.

Strange movie—an Indo fishbowl where Ellis night-surfs for sanity,
He wears clear rubber clown boots, ankles bleeding conceited serenity.

Finless waxless orange Rabbits Foot is tucked beneath my legs, hairy,
"I have same board," nearby Japanese girl says, chewing in meated serenity.

We cuddle and stroll the streets to a barber shop that sells Rabbits Feety,
Behind it we watch a car zoom off a State Park cliff to fleeted serenity.

The driver is Ellis, still in his big clear rubber boots and he is Kew's enemy,
Japanese girl lunges toward him and plunges into the boiled cheated earth.

Serenity.

Make America Shamanistic Again

ginsist

*Heretofore unknown poetic scheme "Ginsist" is my custom phraseologic ode to the spectroscopic axons/dendrites/neurons noodling the cancer-ashed New Yorkonsciousness of ingenious Madeline Gins, prosaist/poet/painter/ philosopher/architect "who publicly forswore mortality and whose buildings were designed to preempt death for those living in them." (–January 2014 *New York Times* obit referencing her Reversible Destiny project.)

These Ginsisms are drip-drip-drip immortal dusts of anxious Kew nightdream, dry windy summerheat reverie, boozy gemthought and lonesomely silent starry New Moon meadowvision of hidden heart all basted and stylized per Gins's pan-CAPS 35-page prose poem leading her gobbledygooky *What The President Will Say and Do!!* (Station Hill Press, 1984)–penned, as *Purplēdeneye* was, while trapped in a toxic Republican-presidential (hers Reagan) reelection pageant.

"This work may be rightly judged to be as predictive as it is prescriptive," Gins prefaced. "Nobody doesn't want a president who is not a shaman."

Do you?

SLURRING RED FRANKENSTEINIAN OAF ON FLOOR OF MY PARENTS' BEDROOM BLOODLESSLY CHAINSAWS HIMSELF IN HALF, HEAD TO TOE, THEN EXPRESSES PRIDE AND RELIEF FOR THINNING WITHOUT DIETING.

BE KIND TO THESE PORTALS OF PROMISE.

PARADISE?

LAMP CLOCK 00:00-03:30 FOR NIGHTLY MIDLIFE CRISES.

PARINIRVANA IN OUR GALACTIC HALO.

MEMORY FIELDS AND CAMPFIRES ON THE SUN.

NIGHTTIME IN JEEP TRAILING SOMEBODY FEARFULLY UP STEEP MUDDY LANE.

PREACHY PALE PROFESSORS WITH LONG PINK BRAIDS.

AGAIN I MISS A GOOD WAVEPOOL SESSION WITH ROSS.

HIT TOPS OF PEOPLES' HEADS WITH HAMMER.

BACKSTABBERS AND ACTUAL STABBINGS.

HIDING FROM I-DON'T-KNOW-WHO.

CAT FOLLOWS ME TO TOILET ON CAMPUS WHERE EVERYONE IS EITHER DEAD OR
BURNING WITH FEVER.

SKA BAND (UNTOUCHABLES?) PERFORMING IN OFFICE BUILDING OF PAGAN
COWORKERS ON CORNER.

CAPILLARY COMPLEXITY OF KLAMATH MOUNTAINS.

COSMIC OCEANS!

PERIMETER OF SELF.

VALE OF QUONDAM SOUL.

GODDESS IN A WHEELCHAIR.

TODAY'S FORECAST: SMOKE.

READ HER DIARY ABOUT SELLING FELLATIO.

REACH NIRVANA!

COOK ISLANDS/'AVAIKI NUI–BLUE BRAIN BANGLE.

SURPRISED BY JOY!

NEW SUMMER.

WORLD MIRRORS!

EVERY RHODODENRON HAS ITS ROSE.

BIG HIGH DRY RIDGETOP INLAND WINDS ROAR FROM KALMIPOSIS AND RIVER
VALLEYS ROGUE PISTOL CHETCO WINCHUCK ON HUGE LOUD SUNNY AIRY
CLEARBELL STOIC REGAL HOLLOWECHO MORNS WHEREIN BIRDSONG AND VAST
FIR PSITHURISMS FUEL ETHER, COMMANDING PRESENCE OF JUNE, FEARS OF
FUTURE FIRES GATHERING AS MOISTURE SEEPS BACK INTO ATMOSFEAR.

OF ONE HEART ONE MIND.

HORROR OF BALDNESS.

HOME HERMITAGE: RIDGE OF RESURRECTION.

LATE-AUGUST PROPHECY OF RIVERBANK ROCKS REARRANGED TO READ "THANK
YOU" IN SWEET PLEASANT WILLOW SHADE.

TINNITUS WILL NEVER ALLOW FOR PURE SILENCE.

BUBBLING SUNSET OF AUGUST: TWILIGHT DRAGONFLIES AND JAZZ SALAD.

AMONGST LATE JUNE GRASSES WAVING IN SOFT WINDS WHILST READING *DORA
LIVES* 'NEATH SUNWARM'D FRAGRANT CEDARS WHILST LYING ON SLICK WHITE
PLASTIC CHAISE LOUNGE SIMILAR TO THE LOUNGE MIKI LAY ON OUTSIDE HIS
PARENTS' MONTECITO COTTAGE AT END OF 2001.

LE POINT VIERGE (T. MERTON)

"SENTIMELANCHOLIA." (CREDIT TO WORD-INVENTOR D. RENSIN, *ALL FOR A FEW
PERFECT WAVES.*)

ANTHROPOMORPHIC LIZARDS ENGAGED IN CANINE COITUS.

HENRY'S TREMENDOUS BODYBOARDING WIPEOUTS IN PERU.

WITH TREVOR LOOKING AT UNDERWATER WAVE FOOTAGE FROM PERU.

OVERWHELMING PARTIES IN UNLIKELY SPOTS—MANY BEAUTIFUL YOUNG WOMEN
& NOAH GETTING DRESSED-UP IN A HOUSE OF CARDS.

FATHER DODGING TAXES IN SUMATRA.

BUTYRACEOUS LAGOON OF WINCHUCK SALMON.

O TERESA! (NOT YOUR MOTHER.)

OLD CARS IN VERMONT & STUDYING WOMEN OF HAIRY ARMPITS.

SILENT ORANGE EYE RAYS OF JULY SUNDOWN COOLDOWN THROUGH OLD LANE-GRACING PINES.

WILD FEELS OF SOCIAL HEART FAILURE.

DUST MOON IN LEMON WATER SINGS WITH DUSK THRUSH (SWAINSON'S) SEEKING NIGHT MATE.

IN DIM PASTEL HAZY FRONT YARD DUSK TWO FOALS NURSE FROM FAWN BETWEEN FLORA FEASTING WHILE I WATCH *SUNSEED* ON QUIET JULIUS CAESAR NIGHTFALL.

"I'LL BE YOUR KNUCKLEHEAD."

WE ARE ALL SECRETS.

WINDY RAINY WILDERNESSES IN SOUTHERN HEMISPHERE WHILE OLIVER SACKS MASSAGES SUPERNOVAE.

NEIGHBOR DAVE USES A TRACTOR TO LIFT HIS RV INTO THE AIR WHILE ADVISING ME TO FLEE TO MENDOCINO AFTER WEDNESDAY BECAUSE THE UTOPIANS WILL CONSUME US—HE ASKS WHETHER MY PROPERTY HAD BEEN SURVEYED AND ASSERTED MOST PROPERTY LINES ARE "TOO STRAIGHT."

YOUNG WOMAN IN MINISKIRT WITH PURPLE CAT AT THE SCHOOL LOCKERS.

AGAIN READING ABOUT MIKI WHILST IT IS AGAIN RAINING DEAD CEDAR SPRIGS UPON MY SLIGHTLY SUNBURNT SKIN.

TAHITIAN BIKINI MODEL FOR HINANO BEER SMILING AND FAMILIAR. SURF-ATTEMPT IN MUTANT COPPER-HUED SLAB WAVES FRONTING HOUSE YARD WHERE WE ARE PLANTING DARLINGTONIA CALIFORNICA.

LOVEFUSION IN THE HOT WINE AFTERNOON.
YOUNG SPANISH GIRL WEARING NO BRA SHAKES HER BREASTS & I HEAR MAMMARY
MILK SLOSHING WITHIN.

FRACTUR'D FROGMAN FRACTAL SHADOW ON NEWTY ALGAL SANDPEBBLE RIVER
FLOOR.
ARGUING WITH AGGRESSIVE WHITE BALD MAN—WE'RE IN WETSUITS—TO THE
SOUP KITCHEN HE HAS BROUGHT WRONG CAKE BATTER.

SMOKY PARTY IN ELEVATOR.

TERRIBLE HAIR CONDITIONER ISSUED ABOARD AIR MARSHALL ISLANDS.
LOITERING AT THE BROOKINGS CAR WASH, I AM PRESIDENT OF RUSSIA TRYING TO
NOT GET TEA-KILLED.

RIPPLES OF COLD SOUTHWIND BREATH ATOP DEAD BROWN FLOATING
BUTTERFLIES.

3 P.M. BIRD-TINKLING HEAT DEAFENS FRAGRANT DUSTY RIDGEWOODS WHILST
WHEELING VULTURES SCRAPE THE SKY.

MARK MCINNIS & I RUSHING AROUND HUGE OREGON CITY OF NEWPORT (IN
REALITY QUITE SMALL) & ALL-NIGHT PARTIES WITH DOZENS OF PEOPLE AFTER WE
SWIM LAPS IN LARGE INDOOR POOL.

A RAIN FESTIVAL WITH BOB WEIR—WE RECITE SONNETS OF SHAKESPEARE—
HIGHLIGHT DRAMAS OF YESTERYEAR.

THINKING OF KURT COBAIN WHILE LAYING IN PEA GRAVEL ABOVE STINKY LOS
ANGELES DRAINAGE DITCH.

AWAKENING IN SOMEBODY'S SLOPED PARK-LIKE FRONT YARD AMID BLUSTERY
MORN.
NANAIMO LOGGER REPEATS "WEE" AND "FRIEND" TO RALLY MOTION SICKNESS
FROM HOGSHEAD OF HALF-CROWN ALE.
CABINS—A LODGE—RUSTIC DARK FOYER & ROOMS—LONG NARROW WALKWAYS
AROUND LAKE AT BOTTOM OF GARDNER RIDGE BUT THERE IS NO LAKE ON THE

RIVER–DESPERATE WIFE WITH HUSBAND FOLLOWING ME TO PLAY CARD GAMES
WITH FEW NICE OLDER COUPLES IN SHADED COOL RELAX'D GREEN AND YELLOW
COUNTRY WOODS, A SCENE WHICH IS A MOVIE SET.
LAYING ON GRASS ASIDE MARK DISCUSSING A FRIEND'S CHARGE OF RAPE.

GAZE LOCKED ACROSS WAVY WINDSWEPT FLAXEN GRASSES FOUR FEET HIGH IN
MY BACKYARD'S EYE.
CHAINSAWING POST-BOTTLE OF WINE– TWO-STROKE DUNGAREE-REEK.
WITH JIM MORRISION IN EUREKA HOSTING DINNER WITH NO FOOD.
IN COLLEGE TRACK TEAM TRYOUT JOGGING WITH NO SHOES.

OCEANS OF EYES.
ORANGE MIDNIGHTING WANING GIBBOUS MOONRISE OVER HUGE NORTHEASTERN
LIGHTNING SMOKE.
WAXY GREEN LEAVES: MADRONE OR MANGO?

JOHNNY'S WIFE AND FRIEND ARE ACTING RUDE AND HAVE TWO LARGE DOGS
TRESPASSING BEYOND BARBED WIRE ON MY EASTERN BACKYARD.
VIRGO'S SUPERNOVA FACTORIES!
MY SISTER HAS GROWN SUDDENLY FROM 5'3" TO 6' IN HEIGHT AND WORKS ASIDE
HUGE FRAYED LIVE WIRE ON REMOTE MISSISSIPPI BEACH.
SENTENCED FOR BEING A SUMMER SLUGABED.

ARID NORTHWEST MOZAMBICAN BORDER IS TWO-INCH-WIDE FINGER-DRAWN
LINE IN SILKY SAND–THERE WITH MY IMMEDIATE FAMILY SNOOPING IN DUSTY
DESERTY HEAT–I YAK WITH HAPPY GANG OF BRIGHTLY-DRESSED ENGLISH-
SPEAKING LOCAL GIRLS AND ONE OF THEM DEEMS ME "A BEAUTIFUL HAWAIIAN"–I
MISS TRAVELING IN JULY.
BUXOM WAITRESS STEALING FRIES FROM MY PLATE.

PRIMSATIC POT PARADISE (RAINBOW'S END) WITH REDFRESH FERRELO
RASPBERRY WINE.

"STAR-SPANGLED BANNER" IN CRISP KNEE-TICKLING AFTERNOON MEADOW OF
HEAVY SILENT ORANGEPURPLE PASTEL HAPPY CAMP BLAZE.

RESPECT TO TOLOWA DEE-NI'.

LUBED CASCADIAN CAROUSAL–NEW YEAR'S DAY–DEEP FRESH SNOW–EVERYONE
HAS PAIRED–SOLE GAL LEFT FOR ME TALL BLONDE & MYSTERIOUSLY SHE SHRINKS
HERSELF 12 INCHES–IN BOURBON BARREL WE TUMBLEDOWN ROCKY SCREE &
ANNOY MORNING PLOW CREW–LATER IN COZY CABIN SPENCER FRIES BACON–
OFFERS US WARM BLACK SPIDER BEER.

EVANESCENT WHITE WINDS OF LOVE.

MOONY SONG SPARROW & JUPITER AT OPPOSITION.

TENDER COMFORT OF MIDSUMMERMIDFALL FIELD CRICKETS.

MORNINGSTAR MARS & ARCING CELESTIAL VISITOR nEAR-eARTH oBJECT wIDE-
fIELD iNFRARED sURVEY eXPLORER.

SERPENT–SPIRAL ROAD–SUSURRATION–GLASS DOOR TO SATURN FUTURE.

ANFRACTUOUS STAGNANT HEATWEEKS–MONOI NIGHTS–SCENTED
CONSCIOUSNESSES–OIL INERTIAS.

SPLINTER'D TIMBERS OF SAD GRISTLY SAN-PEDROISMS DRAWN DOWN INTO
WEIGHT OF MIDSUMMER GRAVITIES SEARED DAY TO DARK–INCENSE OF CONIFER
SINKING INTO FELINE FREEJAZZ FLEA CLEANSINGS AMONG FINE SANTA MARIA
CHARDONNAY & GRILLED CHICKENTITS AMONG LONG YELLOW SLANTS OF
ANGELS AMONG HOLY COOLING WESTWIND MYTHS OF OLD DOUG-FIR STUMP SAP
STUCK TO MY BUTTOCKS.

ANCIENT SUBSURFACE ALIEN OCEAN.

OTHER ARBOR ACQUAINTANCES: CHINQUAPIN–HEMLOCK–MADRONE–ALDER–
MANZANITA–CEDAR–TANOAK. SO?

BLURRED OILY LENSES FREEING OCULAR HEADACHES.

ORANGE CAT ON A HOT WOOD STEP.

CAT ON A HOT SIN REEF.

RECALL *SANTOSHA*.

SATURN AT OPPOSITION–.

WEE WHITE JELLYFISH BLOOM DROOPS FROM CORNJEWEL EYE IN HOPEFUL CLUTCH OF BEE.

NO HOME SHALL CONTAIN LEGAL ELECTRICAL WALL OUTLETS.

MERCURIAL HYPNAGOGIC EPHEMERA.

SUN RA'S DEAD EYES ATWINKLE.

NEURAL HIGHWAYS–DARK EQUATORIAL BELTS.

DOUGLAS-FIR BARK ETCHINGS IN SKY–DINOSAURS & SKELETAL ANATOMY.

MAPFUNO BELOW MIKI DORA.

WALKING THROUGH DEAD WAIST-HIGH GRASS IS THE SWEEPING VOID OF WE.

MEANWHILE IN THE DISTANCE I SEE GREAT FIRE–PROBABLY HOMELY COZY BONFIRE–'XISTING AFORE BANALITY.

SMOKENOSE DAWN IN SECRET ROOSTER SILENCES–RECOLLECTIONS OF PURPLE SUNSETS AT SHELTER COVE.

PAUSE MIDWOMB AMID IRRADIATED ALGAL CHETCO FLOW–GREEN MORNING HEAVEN BENEATH BULLET BOMBAST–NEWT AND CRAWDAD BABES OF STEELHEAD SENSUALITY.

ATOP THE STUMP I BEER-BURP WITH THE FERAL SATURDAY ROOSTER.

AMUSING QUIB READ TODAY– "BEEN MICRODOSING LSD & FAILED TO TEXT HER BACK BECAUSE I LOST MY PHONE."

MAGIC FOR MY FINGERTIPS–FEEL THE EARTH WHEEZE–NEW MOON NIGHT IS ACTIVE CEILING.

AIRPLANE EMITS RAINBOW MACHINERY OF LIGHT WHILST JUPITER FADES TO BLUE.

202: WASHINGTON, D.C.–303: DENVER–404: ATLANTA–505: ALBUQUERQUE– 606: KENTUCKY–707: NORTHWEST CALIFORNIA–808: HAWAI'I–909: SOUTHEAST CALIFORNIA.

INVERT'D DISCS SHIELD SUMMERGRASS FROM ECHOES OF EAST BUT WELCOME ZEITGEBER DIMENSIONS OF TWILIGHT.

SPRUCE CREEK SATURDAY SEPTEMBER SURFPRISE.

AND THEY WOULD SHIP THE TIMBER GRAVEYARD INTO THE SKY AND THE STARS WOULD MOVE AT MY WILL.

KINETIC FIELD OF RED FLAG WARNING–SHY WINDY SOMNAMBULISM FROM SLATER BUTTE RAPIDITY.

TRICKLED STROKE OF MIDNIGHT–LOW MARS MEDITATION LEVITATES FROM KALMIOPSIS IN DIRECT LINE OF SIGHT AMONGST PINEYWOOD CHIPS.

SHAMAN SLIDING IN FROM EAST WITH MILKY WAY–ANCIENT INDIAN VIBES– PATTERNS OF THE SHOOTING STAR–GALAXY SHIFTING IN THE GLOW.

TIME: LEO, 2020. PLACE: CHIT.

NEW MOON: MIRABILIAC THROB OF SILENCE.

WITH MARS AS IT RISES I APOLOGIZE TO YOU.

MY BODY WRITES MY VOICE.

THALASSIC SCAPE TATTOOED BY TIME.

SCENTED AIR & HEAVY HUM OF OREGON'S NOCTURNAL BALCONIES.

ZEN SPONTANEITY AMONG THE LOVED ONES IN GRASS OF PASSION IN THE DRIPPING SPRUCE SHADE OF WORSHIPFUL AUTUMN LIGHT.

MARE NECTARIS. EH?

YOU'RE NOT NORMALLY HUMAN GOOFING IN THE MEADOW WITH A GREAT BEAR INCHING EAST.

HOOT FROM *HOOT* DISTANT *HOOT* FOGHORN *HOOT* AS *HOOT* FOG *HOOT* SLIDES *HOOT* FEATHER'D *HOOT* FINGER *HOOT* UP *HOOT* RIVERVALE.

I'M SLOUCHED ASIDE NEAL CASSADY IN BREAKFAST DINER WHILST ALLENGINSBERG ORALLY REVIEWS PLATES OF FOOD.

NEWMOON ASTROGAZE—PIERCE HEAVEN CONNECT.

GRAVITY IS *DIRECTION*.

"HATRED IS THE UGLY LITTLE DAUGHTER OF THE EVIL WITCH OF IGNORANCE." —VUSAMAZULU CREDO MUTWA

"LIFE IS...PASSING TIME AS GRACEFULLY AS POSSIBLE." —MIKI DORA

Zhuzh the Zen

haibun

Mechanical machinegun rapidity—pileated woodpeckers—raw sonic spring sensations along same rhythms as cats purring—breathing in, out, in, out—resting inside Tuesday blue hour—chasing midnight fissions—subconscious psychvisions of more confusions and misdirections and feeling lost in green mold strangeland but not what it once was—New Zealand or Chile or Yap—tremendously muddy tracks along bare bluffs—bleed to sea—white sneakers on feet of strangers riding strange buses and smashing glass glitter bottles of strange beers in strange houses—chaotic always.

Vernal-dripped Coast Range
Fragrant ferny flowers
Frothings of wet-fringe frights

Ikigai Illusionary

haikuisation

South Padre Island afternoon
Windy beach grass on fire
Watching staticky French TV in my car

"Instapoet" event cybermassacre
71-year-old man is blown-up in Crater Lake
Bloody fatcat glares at my garage

Floating downriverdrunk with Kelly
Gaping at grizzly bears
Burping crocodiles asleep in my house

Spun

irrational sonnet

Televisions scream at us in a dark liquor store,
Scenes of smoky downtown Carlsbad at war—
Façades and marquees, chants from Dead Sea Scrolls.

To the south, hypnotic, fly two translucent Suns:

Incandescence for us to thieve organic souls
Spencer desires to intoxicate with whores,
Gorge on ravens and red wildflower smores
Instead he steals a razor tray of cinnamon rolls.

To the south: diffused, our white Gemini Suns—

Asudden are the booze shelves aflame and I refuse the buns.
I fling them into a trashcan for the Melvins' Buzzo King.
Spencer, outraged, threatens me with two empty guns—
Pistol-whips my fingers with a painterly force that stuns
Buzzo, with his pet bees and tarantula hawk wasp to sting.

Purr Blurr

isonym

"second repeating fast radio burst tracked, deepening mystery" / new earth festival of lights / gurgling creek / cute women hug summery sweat trees / Allen Sarlo hands me a tub containing cream cheese, his signature inscribed / I eye him and ask: "That's it?" / he laughs and walks away / then I'm in car alone driving hyperspeed / supposed to be Medford but miss exit / for 100 miles parallelling road needed / can't reach / everybody's hauling ass loud bright like video game / no pet store errands! / Sun low / afternoon golden day / sudden bird's-eye view from vehicle over Interstate Five / violent motorists weaving cutting zooming darting / generic valley Jackson County landscape blurs past / Kew at beach aside old landlord Kevin / Casie is there fertilizing weeds / guys impress-angling / reality boyfriend stocks Grocery Outlet shelves / leaping into indoor swimming pool-cum-wave pool / grinding right-hand barrel racing acute angle akin Mexican sand point / huge human crowds / abruptly red candles alight, illuminating fact we surfing inside an aquarium / chlorine melts my flesh / skeleton closets unveiled.

The Next Earth

jeremiad

+//+

in solemn Rite Aid checkout line & the store's electricity is dead & the room
is illuminated via dozens of Chinese lanterns stuck to the ceiling looking like
glowing orange jellyfish & an insulting six feet behind me standing on a line of
blue tape is that hot girl Michelle from Ventura whom I knew briefly during the
year 2011. she hands me the apple pie I'd forgotten to include on my shopping
list & someone gets a butcher scale & hooks it to the pie to weigh it & the pie
starts to ooze appley gravy sauce & sausage grease onto the yellow tile floor
& the stagnant air smells of bacon & cigarettes & people start laughing &
somebody asks me "what's your problem, dude?" & suggests I buy 80 acres
on which to farm apples & more people start laughing & a skinny old man who
looks like me at age 80 brings me a newspaper containing property listings
of 80 acres per & his dirty white shirt says BAGEL VISION on the front & he
informs me "this just goes to show you how corrupt realtors because their
apple lands are listed in the paper for years but nobody is eating apples! they're
poisonous, dude!"–

+//+

now absolutely everyone for miles are surely laughing & the pie has become
a swirled floor mound of brown goo identical to the "pile of poo" emoji (but
with no cartoon happyface), so I start to piss on it, & then beautiful shy little
longbrownhaired Michelle, still six feet behind, yells to me that I shouldn't
be exposing myself inside Rite Aid & that for my goopy poo pile of apple pie
I specifically will need paper (plastic is illegal!) bags, the kind with handles,
to scoop & carry it out–she is acting like she knows everything & tries to
micromanage my checkout process but the old germy empty black conveyor
belt & obese black-hooded red-masked sunglassed cashier are now 100 feet
away & Michelle starts to cry & says society is a yellowjacket nest & she runs
out the back door to the asphalt alley gripping her yellow purse bristling with
bottles of coconut shampoo & cosmetics she did not pay for & with a grotesque
thud she is immediately struck & killed by a police car that (like in a movie) had
squealed on two wheels around the building's corner with roof lights aflash

& siren shrieking pursuing two teenage skateboarding looters who were clad
only in white briefs, something I actually did with Kelly when we were teens in
Encinitas 30 years yore—

+//+

once outside (sans pie) I am perplexed by the green tint to my vision so I glance
up & see the Sun is a hot ball of clover & realize today is St. Patrick's & the
vernal equinox is en route & green makes me all a-twitter so gleefully I shuffle
my dead legs to a cliché harborfront Irish bar festooned with papery decor but
there is no one inside, not even a barkeep, so I creep behind the shiny brass
taps & pour myself a few fine pints of Guinness & clink a few rounds of solo
billiards in a smoky red-lighted upstairs room whilst "Magic" (by The Cars,
1984) floats loudly & annoyingly looped from an unseen juke box—

+//+

then I am teleported to my parents' house where there is a sad Christmas tree
& nobody making the fist of usual activities there. the tree (noble fir) weeps
& nothing adorns it & the house is dark & drafty & there's a deep gray storm
approaching but then I'm in Carpinteria trying to surf Rincon but I cannot
find my surfboard nor leash that was broken anyway & I need to ride my bike
& I consider texting ol' Billy so I can enter the precious kingdom & park at
his house but it is starting to rain & it's really windy & at the bottom of the
street of zoom traffic & I almost hit another person also on a bike, this one a
blond woman, & suddenly it's golden sunny & we both end up in a bookstore &
start talking & she tells me her long strange unpronounceable German name
& next we are in an airport & people are getting frustrated trying to get on a
plane & on a television above the podium there is a scene of Chinese satellites
crashing into the Moon & in powdery white mushroom dust—explode!—

+//+

German gal says: "Erde kommt als nächstes"

("Earth is next.")

Swirl

khamriyyat

In the afternoon of Cinco de Mayo a black Welsh girl is downing shots of Mendocino syrah as she violently coughs in an empty Irish bar where there is a high-pressure shower running and she hears wall-pounding and in the room above people are roughly playing musical chairs and slamming things around and yelling threats to mystic Arabic girls doing ballet downstairs along the wet stone lane; they wear their eyeglasses sideways and they peer through cracked street-level windows at the black Welsh girl, deeply contrasted she is against the bright pink walls and steel refrigerators covered with Trump and Bernie stickers and magnets in the attached garage where small cars are parked and it seems to be a suburban stucco townhouse but it's actually this Irish bar in this suburb with a swimming pool next to a dental clinic where my friend Gill and I are arguing with each other about church and the Bible and later I apologize for being a jerk and I leave and when I come back he is roaring drunk in the bar's shower which flows not water but red wine and soon we're again yakking very loudly in the echoey garage amongst the cars and there's a little yellow light in his mouth while he brushes his teeth and the black Welsh girl rushes in and yells at Gill about the shower's wine steam and the steam tells me it is hearing Spanish voices.

Redwooding

kyrielle

In Santa Cruz, chatting with cop
Elevator to mountaintop
For black space-station vibration
At moony sad desolation

Oh, it's called Sun Facility
Overlooked for tranquility
Tallest mountain in the nation
In moony sad desolation

I was fasting in Bonny Doon
Pulling cues from a food cartoon
In a mining operation
Of moony sad desolation

The cop holds qualms with his boyfriend
Who surfs with sharks at town's west end
Winter crystal hibernation
To moony sad desolation

Elevator has weird windows
Long mirrors shaped like panty hose
We drop fast, raw gravitation
From moony sad desolation

Doors yawn wide to street construction
Dozen damn roosters' disruption
Horrific intoxication
With moony sad desolation

Down here I love—I do not live
Stained with fake pains—cannot forgive
Crimson of heartbeat salvation
Face: sad moony desolation

Down here we dream of coral seas
Ravaged trees and dead privacies
We suffer from mood stagnation
All sad moony desolation

Mad at this yet I say nothing
About our liberty crushing
Safety within meditation
Your sad moony desolation

Lobster Caves

limerick

Surfboard auction among alien rat race
Trevor and I smug, sunburnt of face;
Folks roaring drunk
Flower Moon spelunk,
Middle fingers up to shelter-in-place.

Icelnd

lipogram

Siglufjörður—winter solstice, pseudo-sunrise—forthwith there will be no cockcrow nor common morn. No brekkie. Not even brunch of fermented chondrichthyes.

I'm with my longtime illustrious shutterbug friend Chris ("Burkie"), both of us slip-sliding on his preferred silent suite of frozen ponds/inky echoes. Required to help me sketch sublime photos, he promises, of high flowery northern lights over chutes plunging from obscure icebergs—our fuzzed nitrogen-rich glimmers of intense endlessness.

"Let's hug the universe!" he yells, jogging in tight circles, grinning his friendly mischievous cuddly grin. "Seize the night!"

Wistfully I hold one of his numerous iPhone 12s. I'd hoped we would use two of his newest most-expensive mirrorless Sony models but he sternly refused, citing security, which to me seemed preposterous.

But look—beyond the bergs, weird silhouettes lurk mesmerizingly greeny-blue, mixed with purply-pink swirls sweeping the entire fjord. Oddly my phone screen shows colorful (but blurry) shots depicting this cosmic web—of comets, of splotchy orbs.

Chris is beside himself. Eden.

"Wow, it looks like Hubble's Cosmic Reef!" he shouts. "This one here—is it Mercury? Venus? Jupiter? Neptune? *Pluto?*"

"Doubtful," I counter. "Blots of psychedelic poop."

He howls before his oblique jogging resumes. His glee is infectious. His destiny here is imminent. His oily plump cheeks glisten from the dim hue of our modern hyperconnective Cupertino-Shenzen devices.

Like rocketeers, for true effect, one of our spirits must inch closer to the rippling whirling light. Either me or him.

"Kew! Did you know Scott Kelly with Kjell Lindgren recently grew red lettuce on the ISS? Peppers, too! Moony orbiting crops, dude!"

"Selenologic produce? How delicious! Non-GMO, I reckon."

Cosmic lettuce theories now quickly nixed by the brisk mock shutter *click-click-click* of Chris's 12. Fleetingly he's moored his big booted feet; his numbed fingers feverishly compose, focus, execute. Expertly. Coolly. This virtuosic guru of the lens never fizzles nor flops, not even when Chris is cold or lonesome on top of the world. Perfection forms the bedrock of his studio empire down in SLO.

He stops shooting to suggest I view his screen of eos delights. The essence of his work is shocking, humbling, wholly inspiring. The northern lights defined: notoriously tough to reconstruct scenes seen by most eyes of wight. Not Burkie's. His sense my musings by ogling directly into mine.

Yes—he's done it.

Suddenly his 12 bursts into smoke. His skull's two brown oculi explode crosswise like goopy little whizzing flesh rockets which turn purple then turquoise while his densely clothed body dissolves, twisting into something ghostly resembling old night reveries sunken by the side of my synthetic green 1990s college bong long before he—*it?*—is now slowly rising then flying off out over the immense icefield ostensibly en route to our twinkling photobergs, this wild new specterous blur brightly reflected on lonely ice. The glorious northern lights now nestle my old friend, yes, this colorful disk ever yonder, frolicking like dolphins, ether to ether, blended perfectly into this esoteric cosmic kingdom where he'd long, so long, wife or no, sons or no, empire or no, wished to be.

(Now time for lunch.)

text without 'a'

Talons Of

luc-bat

Erin and I browse books
in a spooky death library
Wood shelving, dust fairies
Message on the hairy stone fence
Pancreases are "tense"
We are both doomed, hence must find cure
Costs half-million, sure
We enter an impure school bus
rowdy with filthy cuss
body odor and pus tattoos
Tweakers, nothing to lose
One vomits boozy fizz
One releases orange Fanta whiz
One begins quiz caper
Taps my head with toilet paper
I'm to name vapor (foul)
Erin mutates into an owl

Preppers

melting snowball

polyacetylenes
horticultures
antioxidants
herbivorous
vegetables
potassium
apiaceae
shroomy
garden?
frown
says
god
no
O!

Vernal Rain Evokes Sanguinolency

mesostic

ashley loVed living in england
which was rEally san francisco
but she hadn't lived theRe, either
says it was better thaN attending another college
and hAving sex with hippies
with whom she'd Licked acid....
i had not seen rodgeR in decades
he's become A midget and a bald family man
i compliment him about hIs long-sleeved dress shirt
i Need new clothes....
laura's backyard resemblEs the rockies of banff
she and friend are in bikinis bending oVer
loOking really tan really good
i thinK we're in sonoma, not banff
laura walks into the housE to get something
an invisible woman says "i love you, Slut"....
christmaS eve amongst family in encinitas
time for dessert and i shun dAd's restrictive food rituals
everyone has gone haywire, poiNting at the ruined front yard
Gobs of red balls
i feel absolute rage toward constrUction workers
they broke everythIng
i frowN at them through psychotic eyes
gripping multiple necks while overlOoking the dirt beneath those red balls
they are wrapped in pLastic
i'm lasEred with regret
i want to gNaw red custard or muffins from the jar
but I paniC
seeing someone has lYnched all of mom's horses....

Sprocket and All (By the roan to the contagious hostage)

N+7

By the roan to the contagious hostage
under the surjection of the blue
mottled cloves driven from the
nortripyline—a cold wine. Beyond, the
watchdog of broad, muddy figs
brown with dried weeknights, standing and fallen

patents of standing wattlebird
the scattering of tall trembles

All along the roan the reddish
purplish, forked, upstanding, twiggy
stump of busts and small trembles
with dead, brown lechery under them
leafless vintages—

Lifeless in appendicitis, sluggish
dazed spritzer approaches—

They enter the new worship naked,
cold, uncertain of all
save that they enter. All about them
the cold, familiar winery—

Nubian the graupel, tomorrow
the stiff curmudgeon of wildcarrot leap
One by one obligations are defined—
It quickens: class, outpost of leapfrog

But now the stark dik-dik of
entrance—Still, the profound chanterelle
has come upon them: rooted, they
grip down and begin to awaken

[Per "Spring and All (By the road to the contagious hospital)"
© 1962 William Carlos Williams / New Directions Publishing Corp.]

Celestial Hourglass

nocturne

& Boötes quietly creep-peeps from earlyeast flower sky as wind slinks behind
wuthering murderous sadness in raw realizations of allergic crumblings
'round tragic burnt eyes of the world as waters naturally part in their molds &
they weave & they wove—& wow.

& the wind argues with frogs & silent hazy low sheens / jags in secret fog mists
of the Kalmiopsis & Mount Emily with her clearcuts in the noise of cricket
willows & dew sucking crepuscular realizations knowing nothing is over there
corrupting you besides electric wires & their hopeful progress with stumps
awaiting foxglove nursery in the beauty bounty that can be only springtide.

& to the northeast I admire faintish Ursa Major & my revered winking Leo
constellation at zenith & catstellation Leo minor down dog / down cat! / Spica
smiling here too with metal satellites zooming as moony sky brightens, sinking
into my swollen neck / as the great organic satellite itself glow-hoes from
ancients of ether & unknowingly kisses — nobody really knows, & everybody
knows, & nothing matters — dark matter matters — antimatter matters — wind
matters — yet here again comes the wind — but where is the Moon?

& wind, it licks loudly & loudens & drowns fogs & frogs as Emily crawls closer
evermore & stars present themselves as hot as they can, especially my raw
consolation constellation called Leo. the low hump of Emily, always docile &
commanding overlooking underserving understanding as the full pink Moon
lifts like a nighttime sunrise, a vampire dance with emergence.

& nipple peaktrees of Emily bud bloom bloody bright & brightest like cat
candles or distant doglights of drought discos with survey skins of firs at baselines
whining at everything glowing & going & immediately the frogs begin roaring
as the last little tree tip slips from the bosom — I can see clear boughs now as
the Sun — excuse me! the Moon — makes its first holy presence of pinprick
between peaktrees & suddenly life again flows from universal airs of angst.

Centsorium

nonet

Luscious sensations of memory
Fun farmers market crochet course?
Irish dance class scheduled in
St. Louis, Missouri?
Whimsical road trip—
Gateway Arch, please!
Glencora—
She says
NO!

Fart God

oligogrammatic

Hair of the dog—
Hi there, hater!
Dare to tear a tire for food art?
Oh, good!
Here, rare air for God!
Ha! Arf!
Dote on heft of the irate dog
He ate good arid earth
Afro heart ego—ha!—fair hairdo
Hide? Far road-rage of hot rat or hog
Roar to get goof for their radio
Ah, the oaf of tar toe!
High ire to drag rag hoe!
Fro? Afar—
Ode to eat!
Dig, dig, dig—
or DIE!

Peace Credits

ottava rima

Hopeful sunset bleeds to skull-split morning
Through halls of hatred in suburbia
My feet are drunk, tripping without warning
A pink wolf pounces from dystopia
Fronting Ollie's apartment in Corning
Afraid, I look up to see his wife—*ahhhh*
Plus his pre-teen son behind dusty screen
They frown and glare and slam glass door between

'Round a corner runs a sweating surfer
Blast from past—Luke stops to ask me questions
He startles the wolf which retreats further
He blasts TSOL song "It's Too Late"
He says heartbreak is a form of murder
Yanks his ponytail he's grown for Earth's fate
Whence I rage and delete my parents' trust
Vomit-drooled from vodka pints and youth cuffs:

With Chuck to a dance, we arrived drunky
Pre-blackout, chaperones forced us to leave
We roared up the lane, howling like monkeys
Wove into the path of a cop named Steve
Chuck pissed in Steve's cruiser and puked chunky
Teen goofing—parental stress well-achieved
Thirty years on, I dream of rainbow arcs
Stung by wrong turns and nauseating darks

Wow—Tacocat Radar Sagas!

palindrome

Ah, a bag ban! But civic deed deliver desserts; devil diaper did dim dog; doom drawer emit evil eye; flow gas gel; golf guns; ha! huh!; keels keep knits laced; lager laid; leg level lived; mug nab naps; net nips no noon now; nuts on pals; paws peep pets; pins plug pools; pots rail rats; raw reel refer reward; rotator saw sees sexes slap; sleep smug; snug solos span speed spit; spoons spot star stink; stool stops straw; stressed stun sued tang taps; tide timer tips tit tops; tub warts was won. Now, saw straw, but spot tit spit; remit edit; spat gnat; deus nuts desserts, warts, spots, loots; knits, rats, tops, snoops, tips, deeps, naps, solos, guns, gums, peels, pals sexes sees was rotator; drawer refer leer war; star liar—stop! sloop gulp snip; step peep swap; slap, no stun; won noon on spin; ten span ban gum; devil level gel; dial regal decal; stink peek sleek; huh! ah, snug; flog leg/sag wolf; eye live time reward; mood god mid did repaid lived; stressed reviled deed; civic tub; nab gab—a-ha!

Who?

pangram

Mawky foxshit quelchin' perved jizbag!

Groin Razor

pantoum

I steal a purple house on Florida's Gulf Coast
    Spencer and Britt will arrive with harpoons
From my dock they shall spear fish and sip French roast
    My neighbor'd gifted coffee beans from Cameroon

Spencer and Britt will arrive with harpoons
    Tarpons will soon swarm 'round my wood pilings
My neighbor'd gifted coffee beans from Cameroon
    Once she'd approved my fraudulent tax filings

Tarpons will soon swarm 'round my wood pilings
    Like they do each day of the Sun
Once she approved my fraudulent tax filings
    Neighbor is sunbathing nude, just for fun

Like they do each day of the Sun
    Fish laugh at hooks and the arrogance of man
Neighbor is sunbathing nude, just for fun
    I flyfish and land a sailfish, because I can

Fish laugh at hooks and the arrogance of man
    The harpooners remain casual and nonchalant
I flyfish and land a sailfish, because I can
    Nude neighbor demands I serve at her closed restaurant

The harpooners remain casual and nonchalant
    Now comes Derek, old college friend and musician
Nude neighbor demands I serve at her closed restaurant
    Its architecture is Danish tradition

Now comes Derek, old college friend and musician
    With Sarah, arm-in-arm with the barbarian
Its architecture is Danish tradition
    Sadly for Sarah, its fare is strictly meatatarian

With Sarah, arm-in-arm with the barbarian
    Four nude men arrive and begin to shower
Sadly for Sarah, its fare is strictly meatatarian
    Things are getting weirder by the hour

Four nude men arrive and begin to shower
    Derek is eating raw chunks of tarpon and sailfish
Things are getting weirder by the hour
    Derek finds a banjo and asks me to make a wish

Derek is eating raw chunks of tarpon and sailfish
    In the heat I'm waxing irritated
Derek finds a banjo and asks me to make a wish
    With a question: "Are you constipated?"

In the heat I'm waxing irritated
    A noisy old ice cream truck parks on my dock
With a question: "Are you constipated?"
    While Sarah is yelling at Derek about his cock

A noisy old ice cream truck parks on my dock
    Boiled-red driver is oddly aggressive
While Sarah is yelling at Derek about his cock
    The topic of food has become oppressive

Boiled-red driver is oddly aggressive
 He laughs and leaves bloody ribs from a giraffe
The topic of food has become oppressive
 Ice cream man flings forth a gator that's cut in half

He laughs and leaves bloody ribs from a giraffe
 I hear children yelling from the hidden preschool
Ice cream man flings forth a gator that's cut in half
 Nude Derek jogs and leaps into my swimming pool

I hear children yelling from the hidden preschool
 Loud screams from my backyard shed
Nude Derek jogs and leaps into my swimming pool
 On the bottom he sees Britt and Spencer dead

Loud screams from my backyard shed
 Sarah runs and belly-flops onto Derek's bleeding back
On the bottom he sees Britt and Spencer dead
 Ice cream man stabs me with piece of giraffe rack

Cat Dub

quatorzain

Walking on a wet street in a small town
 East African or Caribbean
 Lovely faces, not a frown
 Nature of time, nectarean
A shaman boils meat over propane flame
 My felonious friend Mark meditates nearby
 In women's clothes, he resembles a dame
 Gazes at me through his sweet third eye
A flower maiden wafts incense to my brain
 Sandalwood for panoramic awareness
 Above me, nymphs chant to the rain
With pangs of thrill and intrigue and desire
 I press boiled meat onto my heart
 Shaman thunders a tremendous fart

Artery

quenina

Dazzling butterflies burp blue rain jewels
Internal currents are soaked with sage sharky surf
My reveries here aside the babbling Big Flat River
Foremostly a fishy creek under the holy Sun
Its coast: scented oil for sanctuary cure
{In lostness I had misplaced this quantum cranial cure
Where I could always walk atop a jittery path of jewels
Footfalls (falling forward) where in fall it is always sunny
From the ass of the wrong foreland at last I step to surf
Fording several raw eager ravenous wilderness rivers
{Mud is my misty memory of the Flat's southernmost river
From the north I see desert mirages, sparkling fruit of the Sun
Mountains and gulches, all too low but instilling a high cure
I soar across a few waves and summon this beloved jade jewel
Then a bearded park ranger creeps to me following celestial surf
{He tells me this land was once part of Sweden, scilicet bad surf
Reckons he regularly raved with LSD at Reggae on the River
And ogled an oversexed Swedish fish gypsy named Jewel
Annoyingly uses his old iPhone to anoint a Tinder cure
Yells he was once a UPS driver on yellow Sundays
{Boasts he was a bawdy beach barkeep throughout the six other sins of Sun
Hooking cold drippy wetsuits to drippy pub gutters before peddling his cures
Aside the gummy gloomy spit-stained boardwalk which skaters would surf
"Rotgut flowed fresh like big bear crap, boy, inna thatta Big Flat River—"
The bearded ranger is vaporized by a suburban rain of jewels
{Now newly dead Oliver Sacks and I debate beards—they *should* cure bad surf
His jewellike green eyes mirror the tall Sun here at the final red shore
Here, indeed, aside his tragic tender "river of consciousness"

Burnshadows

rann

Pink Moon fly in ancient earth fir
Pink Moon exhale tear of feather myrrh
Pink Moon light trail of rooster roar
Pink Moon flood in silent dark gore

Flower Moon, tranquil steady suspended hum
Flower Moon, frogs rise from Emily bosom
Flower Moon, grass residue from heat of day
Flower Moon, fragrant hole in candy skies of May

Strawberry Moon freed from clutter clutch of boughs
Strawberry Moon hopeful crickets from day and drowse
Strawberry Moon dampens dusk on nose of spring
Strawberry Moon illuminates secret worlds again

Tuxedo Fur

rhopalic

black
cats
in a
cloud in
Summerland
lick my feet;
Scott has been mad
for weeks scheming
to rob a moonshine
distillery which
I find odd as there are
no distilleries here;
in a nearby dumpster he
has just had sex with a young
Asian woman who looks like a
geek; he is aloof and kite-high
blabbering about Chicago guns
and strong LSD for Thanksgiving,
his beard greasy from mossy cold pizza;
my mom appears and I suggest we sow
carrots in the Summerland airport's dumpster;
she spits and insists carrots require too much
electricity to grow and all seeds would be
exhumed by black cats on grass of a glass Eden

GP Weather Conspiracy

sestanagramina

Whee! The wet spring Earth!
She cares to paw what heat?
She throws ionic hate into what air?
Ah, she opines with wrath's rain
Rips arcs in ice
On acres in grape water

Her canoe is an oasis on green water
Iris thaws here on the cat Earth
Oceanic noise paws the ice
To eat pecan pie I reheat
Trees in sap rain
To gather crisp irie air

Origins as air?
Sin water!
Sane rain?
Cancer Earth!
Spa heat?
Corpse ice!

Hot crops scare this ice
Raw scars trap the air
Oh, so ironic in the rising heat!
Three scenarios, no water
Ah, so the precision ring IS Earth!
Where is her awe, her rage, her ether rain?

Roses praise the art in rain
Groan on aspiring ices
Sting wheat eaters on Earth
Soar as canopies in the air
Soap the sea waters
Pipe the heat

Oh, how she praises heat!
Wraps ears in rain
Hears the opera as tear water
Her arson to ice
Go sweet, organic spring air—
Is this One Earth?

She ropes the new heat, censors the era's ice
Her cats hate rain (not hot air)
Sowing air water in 2020 = Acne Earth

Stripped

tanka

SHAMROCK

Hillock, huge fight scene
Classic severe drunkenness
Even a romance
Something about me writing
Irish cowboy pulp

SANGUINE

Red owl claws my face
Childhood's red Gabriel rain
Braided blood bondage
Five-a.m. blinding lightning
Thunder ear-split—I'm awake

SAPPHIRE

Dawn's white-crowned sparrow
Sings to flicker and robin
Soothing Swainson's thrush
Hum of madrone universe
Harmony greets quail today

Arab's Alcohol

tautogram

Arms akimbo, Adam awkwardly advances across abundant Armenian acreage, an astonishing apple, apricot, and avocado array amongst annihilated airplanes and ancient automobiles.

Alert and animated, area artist/agronomist/ayatollah Abdul applauds.

"*Alright!* Absolutely awesome, amigo!"

An accomplished Ashkenazi acrylicist, Adam avoids atrocious acts— adultery, alcoholism, animal abuse, arson, assault—alongside any argument against aspiring activists, attorneys, actors, astronauts, African athletes, and avocado aficionados. After all, avocados are angelic agents.

Apex agriculture? *Ahem.*

Always ambivalent, Abdul approves.

"Adorable!"

"An agrestal artform!" adds Adam, assessing and arranging an avocado aside an aged apricot. Altogether admirable and appetizing, avocados augment all Armenian afternoons.

Amazingly, Abdul awards apples and apricots—and an aubergine!— anytime artists arrive aroused and are at all available.

"Ah, aubergine?" an askance Adam asks.

"Amateurish adolescent amusement," Abdul answers arrogantly.

"Auspicious, also."

"Ambiguous. Apparently afraid, Adam?"

"Always abstain! Aubergines are abstract anal aphrodisiacs."

"Appalling and absurd," Abdul announces. "Anyone abnormal advertises aubergines as appropriate."

"Are aubergine applications acceptable *anywhere?*" asks Adam, almost annoyed. "America?"

"Australia."

"Apt. Australians act awfully American, anyhow."

After awhile, applying an actual avocado, Adam's aesthetic acumen accelerates at an alarming angle among acclaimed artwork assemblages, again announcing: "All agrarian art abides! Accolades actively abound across Albania and Algeria!"

"Attaboy," an agog Abdul adds affably. "Apricot-accented avocado art attracts academics across Asia, also, accommodating ambitious and affluent absinthe adventurers at Azerbaijani and Afghani *auberges*."

"Aubergines?" asks Adam, absorbed.

"*Auberges*, asshole!"

Abruptly anxious, Adam alights anon as Abdul, again alone, analyzes— ah, admires!—Adam's abandoned artwork, abstrusely achieving an ascendant appreciation.

"Ambrosial and authentic," Abdul admits, acquiring an apparent awakening, amorous and adrift amongst alien Ashkenazi allure, aloud announcing: "Allah! Abolish *all* aubergines! Allah! Allah! Allah! Avocados are angelic! Avocados are angelic! AVOCADOS ARE ANGELS!"

Anyway....

Dancing Eyelds

tetractys

I
had a
dream about
my prior dream
care for coffee, mr. Freud, mr. Jung?

Dan
posts a
video
S.D. logging
But there is no timber in Point Loma

near
my house
cul-de-sac
a white-robed cop
flashes me; his penis is a pistol

drunk
girlfriend
festival
apathetic
nigh semiautobiographical

wrong
supper
gelatin
hypothermic
you should never eat ice cream with Jell-O

Kinhin Kink

univocalic

Dim drizzly twilight. Whirling windchill. Visibility is nil. Virginity is tricky.

Six psychic hitchhiking Hindis find stylish gypsy chicks singing, stripping itty-bitty bikinis, sinking firm dirty hick dicks, rhythmic, dipping fittingly, vilifying milky tit midwiving childbirths in sticky filthy cribs.

Swigging his Irish whisky fifth, nihilistic pilgrim cycling in slimy miniskirt skids stiffly, flings icy limp kingfish.

Ick!

Irking incivility!

Hicks: "Witchy nitwit!"

Skirmish stirring. First, nibbling spicy pigskin rinds, zitty tinsmith hints: "Lynching? Shiv knifing?" Wimpy millwright clicks in, high, whiffing slim spliffs.

Skipping invincibly, tipsy pilgrim cyclist (with stinky fish tins) simply trips victims whilst striving twixt ditch + sizzling gristmill kiln.

Twin killings!

Hiding, Hindi psychics giggle priggishly. Wilting dirty dicks dribble.

"Grisly hijinks? Nifty!" pilgrim insists whilst grinning, libidinizing. "I'm giddy! Jiving frisky, gypsy chicks?"

Brimming with bliss, this wild misfit triptych drinks gin/whisky mix, strips bikinis till midnight, whistling and licking in Mississippi mists, pinging nippily, living mysticly.

Green Campfire Wine

villanelle

spirit surfsearch on hip of Pangaea
strange sojourn to clove isle of Zanzibar
soundtracked with Rob and Jerry's "Althea"

dire wolf in the high Santa Lucias
bleeding paranoia in Côte d'Ivoire
spirit surfsearch on hip of Pangaea

secrets of cycling west from Goleta
to seaside coves of social reservoir
soundtracked with Rob's and Jerry's "Althea"

Isla Vista seabreeze of tortillas
the world a curious new morning star
spirit surfsearch on hip of Pangaea

brown milk jetty wedge of Nigeria
where brothers surf, no fear of police car
soundtracked with Rob and Jerry's "Althea"

i'm frightened by heat equatoria
domestic Big Sur coast with Jen sweetheart
spirit surfsearch on hip of Pangaea
soundtracked with Rob and Jerry's "Althea"

Sea of Cactus

wasf

2 a.m.—prickly black fogs of your town
run past sawmill one mile east of your beach
hurl huge deathknife at log truck bearing down
pop trailer's bald tires, logs plunge with foul screech

                rainy day, hippie group of knife throwers
                mainly thrusting long knives at moving cars
                hashing silent rage, demonleaf blowers
                for us, bloody suicide behind bars

knives most effective when used in pink light
or near flowers among trees in cloud frowns
quarrel with joggers whose teeth are too white
run very fast from them through small wine towns

                holding low fearsome knife pointed forward
                path through more joggers of rancid perfume
                I feel unstoppable, running northward
                sweating from regret that I've frightened—whom?

I meet young Mexican cowboy who grunts
"el mejor color es el tequila"
his white dog Toni smokes a cactus blunt
is chewed by Elysian monster Gila

                veterinarian, she's a stern bitch
                Mexican cowboy, he tries to impress
                chases her into mill's dark drainage ditch
                forgets his dog's fatal oozing abscess

tickets to see Hawai'ian reggae band
and taco match handed to vet and me
so cowboy can bury poor dog in sand
you brandish huge deathknife so I must flee
your girlfriend was the crashed log truck's driver
bizarre for joggers to cause such mayhem
like cowboy's dog, she was no survivor
so we chew canine tacos—2 p.m.

Xanadu Youth Zeal

X mistakes Y for Z

Bud is convinced Rose, his most recent ex-girlfriend, is in love with Krystal, ex-girlfriend of Michael (a neighbor). Rose thinks Bud is in love with Michael, who Krystal is in love with, unbeknownst to Michael. Krystal thinks Michael is still in love with Rose despite him having actually never loved her. Bud, who often steals Michael's clothes to wear, thinks Michael is out to sabotage Bud's plan to seduce Krystal and make Rose jealous with rage despite she having never loved Bud. In fact, Rose hopes Bud and Krystal will bond so Bud will stop sending dirty texts to Rose's phone. Michael thinks Krystal is in love with Bud despite Krystal actually being in love with Rose and Michael is in love with Bud.

Stewarts Point

yuugen

prior landlord Steve & I
violently wheeze
from rosemary cigarettes
he is old wino
I am new winedrunk
zooming through Mendonoma
in brown filthy 1983 Dodge Caravan
we enter sheriff's DUI checkpoint
are viewed with suspicion
en route to red barn in Sea Ranch
to whittle
(using miniature chainsaws)
cartoon character faces in redwood logs
firstly I am to meet old surfer
who lives in town called Zez
Steve drops me at Timber Cove restaurant
the surfer
(who precisely resembles Ken Babbs)
& I discuss local reefs
he mentions my Mendonoma photos
printed in old surfing magazine
I inform him I've quit photography
we celebrate this
louder & louder are the restaurant voices
we relocate & sit fireside outside
facing four Germans
we chew five fatty steaks & clink wine glasses
meander through further fine talks
reminiscing about my Mendonoma zen journeys
& shambolic moods

asserting I must return to Steve
to carve pieces of Gualala redwood
but Steve does not return
early eve
the fire feels hotter
& hotter
sweating, I look at my iPhone
a cryptic email from Ken Babbs:
"Michael, I am of no chapbooks right now,
    awaiting a new tree.
    be soon."

Smiling Purpluddha

zejel

tiny minds rustle dead meadow grass on my lonesome tinnitus ear
chill heaves down from smokehazed Kalmiopsis grandeur
and ominous Arsia Mons Elongated Cloud, it doth weep near
{holy grandmother seen in Arcturus wink
pondering my father whose blood I drink
feeling his universal sorrows sink
crack'd open by Perseids protean spear
{late-fire August corn now halfway to harvest Moon
Snyder's berry feast & McClure's blackberries bloom
4 a.m. bright Venus katydids crickets flood my blue room
'ere wheeling south—rivermouth at 5 a.m.—'79 year
{meet comity in small crisp surf at Pickleweed Point
with twinkling old kneeboarder who's smoking a joint
into our friendly vision wings a spool of gulls aroint
outflown by osprey who's clawing fish not fear
{white cycloid scales glist—body limp—raptorial shriek
skims phantom sea stacks hoven to tiny minds antique
swoops upriver, away from dark nausea, oceanic mystique
cool jade swimmers' membrane—my neural frontier
{'neath semiautomatic arms ambience—hot myrtle romance
wind evicts deaths of tanoak maple madrone—tragic dance
forward cold browny-white windwhipp'd sea trance
dizzy in river womb I driftsleep—amniotic silken sphere
{frenzied social dreaming again—Milky Way bared to ills of Earth
panicked pantheistic dusk—throbb'd red breath haze—death to birth
Mars, Leo, Pleiades, Cassiopeia zenith—hypnagogic worth
my eyes explode—tiny smiling buddha bubbling clear

Kew first tapped his writerly destiny as a Californian boy in the mid-1980s. His work has since been featured globally in magazines, newspapers, films, websites, advertisements, and books, including January 2012's *Crossings*, his first collection of world travel essays. *Rainbownesia*, his Oceania travel volume, was published in October 2019. In March 2020 he published *Nectars of Sky*, his premier poetry collection, surrealist free-verse based on his two most transformative residencies. Today Kew dwells and delves at Purplēdeneye in the coastal mountains of southern Oregon.